Happy
Divali
The festival of lights

WAYLAND
www.waylandbooks.co.uk

First published in 2016 by Wayland
© Wayland 2016

Written by Joyce Bentley

Editorial consultant: Anita Ganeri
Editor: Corinne Lucas
Designer: Ariadne Ward

A catalogue for this title is
available from the British Library

ISBN: 978 0 7502 9566 6

10 9 8 7 6 5 4 3 2 1

Wayland
An imprint of
Hachette Children's Books
Part of Hodder & Stoughton
Carmelite House
50 Victoria Embankment
London, EC4Y 0DZ

An Hachette UK Company
www.hachette.co.uk
www.hachettechildrens.co.uk

Printed in China

Picture credits: cover photograph © IndiaPicture/Alamy Stock Photo; p 4–5 ©
imagedb.com/Shutterstock; p5 © tjasam/Shutterstock; p 6 © Irisimchik/Shutterstock;
p 7 © Philippe Lissac; p 8–9 © Pete Burana/Shutterstock.com; p 9 © OLI SCARFF/
Stringer; p 10 © stockillustration/Shutterstock; p 11 © stockillustration/Shutterstock;
p 12 © Dinodia/Corbis; p 13 © SANJEEV GUPTA/epa/Corbis; p 14 © IndiaPicture/
Alamy Stock Photo; p 15 © Chris Hellier/Corbis; p 16 © Michael Heiman/Staff/Getty;
p 17 © Chris Hellier/Corbis; p 18 © K. M. Asad/Demotix/Corbis; p 19 © Pacific Press/
Corbis; p 20 © NOAH SEELAM/Stringer; p 20–21 © SANJEEV GUPTA/epa/Corbis; p 22
© Dinodia/Corbis; p 23 © Grant Faint.

Background images and other graphic elements courtesy of Shutterstock.com.

Contents

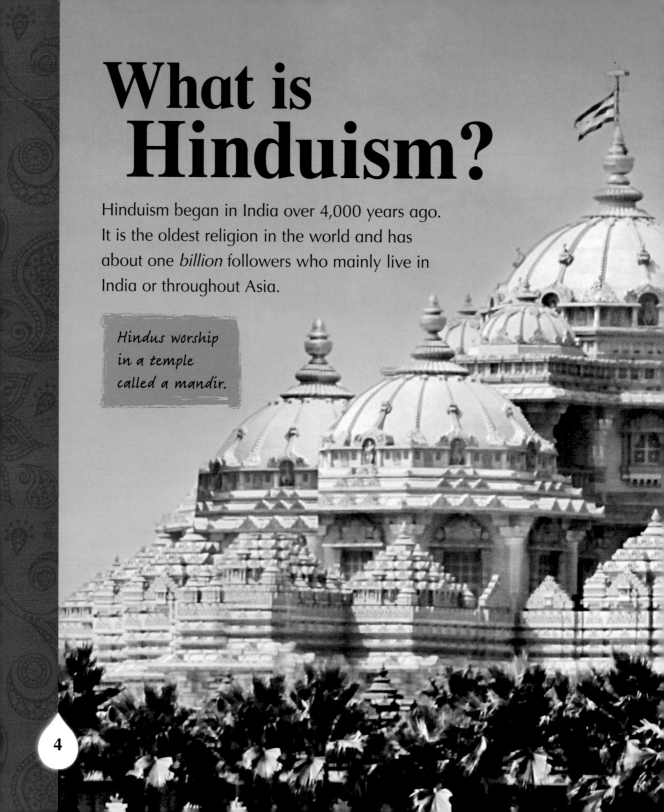

What is Hinduism?

Hinduism began in India over 4,000 years ago. It is the oldest religion in the world and has about one *billion* followers who mainly live in India or throughout Asia.

Hindus worship in a temple called a mandir.

4

Hindus believe in a great soul or spirit, called *Brahman*. Some Hindus worship Brahman as God. For Hindus, Brahman is the power behind everything in the universe. Hindus worship Brahman in many forms, through many different gods and goddesses.

Om is a sacred sound Hindus make. It is chanted at the beginning and end of prayers and during meditation.

Most Hindu homes also have a shrine where people can worship.

5

Hindu Gods and Goddesses

Hindus believe in many different gods and goddesses who represent Brahman's different powers. Three of the most important gods are:

Brahma – the creator
Vishnu – the preserver
Shiva – the destroyer

There are hundreds of gods and goddesses in Hinduism.

Vishnu

Shiva

Brahma

Lakshmi

Ganesh

Saraswathi

The most popular gods in Hinduism are Rama and Krishna. They are forms of the god Vishnu. Hindus do not worship all of the gods. Many have a favourite god or goddess who is special to the place they live or to their family.

Popular Hindu gods

Ganesh – god of knowledge, luck and success

Hanuman – the monkey god, a *symbol* of strength and *devotion*

Krishna – is one of the forms of Vishnu

Lakshmi – goddess of wealth, *prosperity* and beauty

Rama – is one of the forms of Vishnu and is a symbol of *virtue*

Saraswathi – is the goddess of knowledge and learning

Happy Divali

Divali is the festival of lights, which is celebrated in October or November by Hindus around the world. There are many reasons for celebrating Divali. It marks the Hindu New Year and also remembers times in the lives of the Hindu gods and goddesses.

Divali is also called:
Deepavali
Diwali
Dipavali
Dewali

Mumbai train station in India lit up with multi-coloured lights during Divali.

8

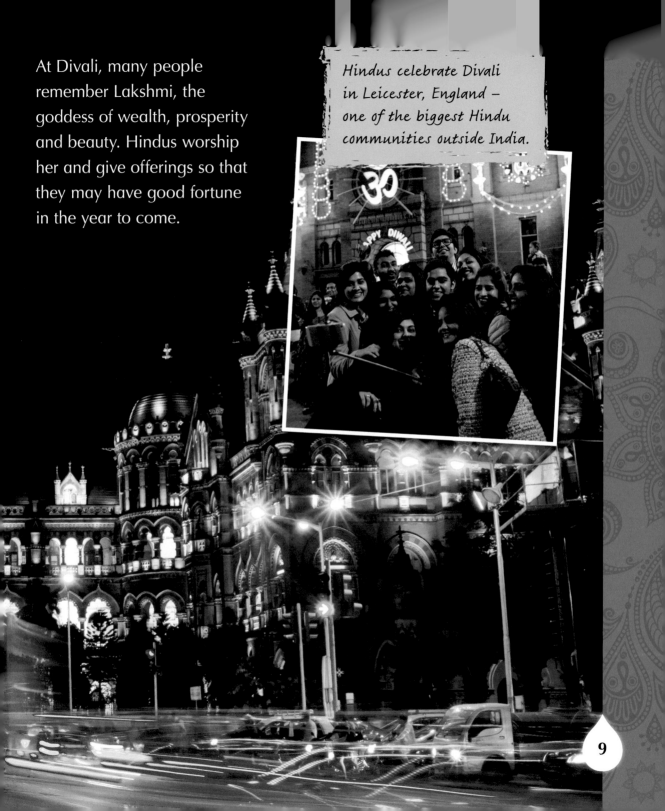

At Divali, many people remember Lakshmi, the goddess of wealth, prosperity and beauty. Hindus worship her and give offerings so that they may have good fortune in the year to come.

Hindus celebrate Divali in Leicester, England – one of the biggest Hindu communities outside India.

The Legend of the
Ramayana

Hindus tell many stories about Divali. The most popular ones comes from a long poem, called the *Ramayana*.

The Poem of the Ramayana

King Dasharatha of Ayodhya had three wives and two sons. Knowing that his *reign* was near its end he looked to his eldest son, Rama, to take over the throne. However the king's wife, Kaikeyi, reminded him of the two wishes he had granted

The mighty monkey god, Hanuman.

her – to put her son Bharata on the throne and to banish Rama. The King reluctantly agreed and so Rama, with his wife Sita and brother Lakshamana, were banished from the kingdom to live in the forest.

After a 14 long years in *exile*, Sita was kidnapped by the ten-headed demon Ravana who took her back to Lanka,

Ravana, the evil ten-headed demon.

where he ruled. Rama asked the monkey god, Hanuman, to help him rescue Sita and together, with Hanuman's monkey army, they killed Ravana and brought Sita back. When they returned to Ayodhya, people lit rows of lamps to guide Rama and Sita back home. Bharata gave up the throne and Rama was crowned king. Today Rama is worshipped for his courage and *devotion*.

Rama goes into battle to free Sita.

Preparing for Divali

There is much excitement leading up to Divali. In some places, Divali lasts for five days. In others, it takes place over a weekend. People clean their houses and go shopping to buy new clothes and gifts for friends and relatives. They also create beautiful *rangoli* patterns on floors and walls.

Colourful rangoli designs are traditionally made out of rice and coloured powder.

Delicious sweets and homemade foods are prepared. Mithai, sweets, are by far the most popular food eaten during the festival. They are given as offerings to welcome the goddess Lakshmi, and as gifts.

Greeting cards are sent to wish people 'Happy Divali'.

Galub jamun, burfi and ladoo are popular mithai.

Lighting the way for Lakshmi

Lights called divas fill houses, shops and public spaces across towns and cities celebrating Divali. People light rows of divas to welcome Lakshmi into their homes, to bring good luck, and to guide Rama and Sita home. Lights burn all night so that Lakshmi will feel welcome and enter at any time. Firecrackers and fireworks go off to ward off evil spirits.

Diva lights also show how goodness drives away evil.

Fireworks light up the sky over New York, during the yearly Divali celebrations.

15

Time for Prayer

At Divali, many Hindus go to a temple to worship the gods and goddesses, and make offerings of food, fruit and flowers. This is called *puja*.

South African Hindus praying to the goddess Lakshmi.

Lakshmi puja is an important ritual performed during Divali. Hindus offer prayers, repeat sacred words and sing as part of the puja. They hope that Lakshmi will bring peace and wealth to their homes and businesses.

During Divali, children are given gifts of new clothes.

Children dress up in red and gold, the colours worn by Lakshmi.

A Joyous Time

Divali is a time for sharing with loved ones. Hindus feast on the special food that has been prepared and give gifts, such as sweets, money and jewellery. People gather to see plays and dances telling the story of the Ramayana, while parties are held for families to come together.

Children light sparklers to celebrate the homecoming of Rama and Sita.

Actors perform Ramlila, a play about the legend of the Ramayana.

Bal Hanuman is a popular children's animated film about the Ramayana.

Thinking About Divali

Fireworks and lanterns light up the night sky to bring Divali to an end for another year. It is a happy time of the year for Hindus with plenty to celebrate, and a blessed and prosperous new year to look forward to.

Hindu women light up the entrance to their home with sparklers during Divali.

om
fireworks Hanuman
Ramayana lotus
sweets Rama Brahman
divas Divali puja
Ganesh Hindu happiness
Lakshmi family
prosperity rangoli
lights Sita

This word cloud contains words that remind us of Divali. Can you think of any more?

Divali is over for another year – Happy Divali!

Design a Rangoli

Rangoli are made on floors and walls to decorate homes during festivals and special occasions. They are beautiful *geometric* patterns made using coloured dyes. The *symmetry* of the designs makes them welcoming and peaceful for any visitor.

Indians use brightly coloured dyes made of rice flour.

Try copying one of these simple patterns to create a rangoli.

Materials

You will need a cake board, plain paper, PVA glue, a pencil, vegetable oil and paint powder.

Getting started

To start, paste plain paper on to a medium-sized cake board using PVA glue. Next, draw your design on the board with a pencil. Cover the paper in a thin layer of vegetable oil, then you can colour in the pattern.

To do this, take a large pinch of coloured paint powder between your thumb and forefinger. Carefully sprinkle the paint powder around the outline of your pattern with one colour, then fill in the shapes with another colour. You can also use other things to decorate your rangoli…

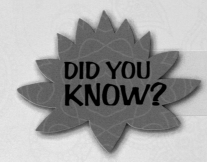

DID YOU KNOW?

Rangoli means row of colours.

Rangoli are often decorated with divas.

spices • cumin • fennel
seeds • tea • leaves • rice
grains • pulses • wheat
flowers • petals • sand

23

Glossary

Billion – a million millions

Brahman – one supreme God

Community – a social group of people living in the same area

Devotion – love and loyalty for a person or activity

Exile – to be forced to leave your country

Geometric – having regular lines and shapes

Legend – a traditional story from history

Meditation – to focus the mind for religious or relaxation purposes

Prosperity – to have wealth

Puja – the act of worshipping a god

Ramayana – a play of the life of Rama

Rangoli – an Indian decoration using coloured rice powder to create patterns

Reign – the period of time that a king or queen rules a country

Symbol – a shape or sign to mean something

Symmetry – when two sides of something are balanced

Virtue – goodness and honesty

Index